THE MAGNA CHARTA OF THE CHRISTIAN CHURCH

by

Karl Friedrich Althoff

Translation by Werner Grimm

Translated from the "Mitteilungen aus der
Anthroposophischen Arbeit in Deutschland" —
No. 132/1980 with kind permission

ISBN 0-919924-15-8

PRINTED IN CANADA

Matthew 16, 13-20

"When Jesus came into the coasts of Caesarea Philippi, he
asked his disciples, saying, Whom do men say that I the Son
of man am?
And they said, Some say that thou art John the Baptist; some,
Elias; and others, Jeremias, or one of the prophets.
He saith unto them, But whom say ye that I am?
And Simon Peter answered and said, Thou art the Christ, the
Son of the living God.
And Jesus answered and said unto him, Blessed art thou, Simon
Bar-jona: for flesh and blood hath not revealed it unto thee,
but my Father which is in heaven.
And I say also unto thee, That thou art Peter, and upon this
rock I will build my church; and the gates of hell shall not
prevail against it.
And I will give unto thee the keys of the kingdom of heaven:
and whatsoever thou shalt bind on earth shall be bound in
heaven: and whatsoever thou shalt loose on earth shall be
loosed in heaven.
Then charged he his disciples that they should tell no man
that he was Jesus the Christ."

Ormond Edwards has published a magnificent little book of
only 90 pages: "A new chronology of the Gospels" (Floris Books,
Edinburgh,1972). In this he substantiates, through exact scien-
tific research of the astronomical and calendaric facts and
through a new evaluation of the historic sources as well as of
the traditions of the old church, what should also be important for our thoughts - and that is: The "Three years" of the
life of Christ are such, that they each are actually of nine
months duration - i.e. the timespan of Man's embryonic development - and this in such a way that each is introduced by a
direction - giving events in Christ's life:

The first, the "quiet year" is introduced by Christ's
incarnation into the earthly body of Jesus at the Baptism in
the Jordan, on January 6, 31 according to our calendar.

The second, the "Galilean year" is introduced by the beginning of Jesus' public work through speaking in the synagogue
at Nazareth on October 6, 31 (Luke 4,15-21);

The third and last year begins with the event of Caesarea
Philippi, with the confession of Peter and the promise that
the Church was to be built on the rock, on July 6,32 - nine
months before the concluding event of the resurrection on
April 5,33 .

I.

Let us be deeply conscious of the fact, that on that
Sunday, July 6,32 the conception, as it were, of that Being
took place, which later as the church was born into the world
and furthermore that this conception came about through that
central conceptual act of cognition, that lightning-like im-
pact of cognition, which opened Peter's inner eye for just

one moment: SY EI HO CHRISTOS! YOU ARE THE CHRIST! The entire development of that mystery drama, presented in the Gospel according to Matthew as Peter's path of initiation, aims for this one meteoric hour when for a cosmic moment from the secretly opening heaven that spirit lightning flames through the night of earth.

What happened during the previous, the "Galilean year"? In April 32 John the Baptist was beheaded. Important events followed which show how the individuality of John from the worlds beyond death worked for the forming of the coming Christ - Community to be the seed of a new world of Man. This we experience at the Feeding of the five thousand and the four thousand.

Immediately prior to this, however, the two leading re- ligious orders speak: the strictly conservative Pharisees and the liberal-progressive Sadducees. They ask the Rabbi of Nazareth for a spirit sign which would legitimize himself before their eyes and ears as authoritative spiritual teacher. This He rejects: "An evil and adulterous generation seeks for a sign, but no sign shall be given to it except the sign of Jonah." (Matt.16,4)

The sign of Jonah, a sign which Christ was to fulfil through His death in the heart of the earth and His resurrection three days later as the "I" of the earth. No other sign but the sign of Jonah! This answer reveals Christ's full rejection of the nationalistic way of thinking of the Pharisees of all ages, but also of the agnostic thought form of the Sadducees of all times.

Now this answer exists on earth; it travels with Him when, on the path to the far north of the country, He teaches His spirit disciples about ideological aberrations which, like a corrupting sour-dough, threaten to permeate and collectivize man's thinking,feeling and willing (Matt.16,5-12).

4.

II.

Where does He go with His disciples? Well, for today's
consciousness the name of Caesarea Philippi does not mean
much. But one should understand that the entire perimeter of
the Roman Empire was covered by a network of sanctuaries, of
temples, dedicated to the emperor, the highes divine lord of
the world. Absolute power of the state was based on submission
to the concept that in Caesar, the emperor, the whole world
of the gods is present and can be worshipped. As an indivi-
dual you may turn to any divinity whom you know, but in the
emperor lives the entire world of the gods, and this demands
your highest worship. This worship requires that grain of incense which you have to cast into the sacrificial flame on
the altar of Caesar!

Think of what the first Christians took on themselves in
refusing just that grain of incense! To swim with the current
and thus keep one's life would have been so easy and simple!
But the word of Solzhenitsyn is valid at any time: Only dead
fish swim with the current, living ones against it.

Caesarea Philippi high up in the Hermon mountains built
by Herod the Great, the alien king of Judea by the grace of
Rome, for the adoration of the divine Augustus, extended for
Emperor Tiberius by Phillippus, the son of Herod, the husband
of Salome, was so to speak the imperial sanctuary "authorized"
for Israel. There Jesus the Christ leads His spirit disciples
not to the temple of Jahve in Jerusalem. It is, as if, by
slipping into his skin, He took up the fight with the dragon.

Now what happens there? Let us hear the Gospel and let us
hear it as antithesis to the outer world.

Up there, on lofty heights, visible for all eyes (which
in any case perceive the visible only) the temple of the
Ruler of the World with continously changing names; down here,
before the entrance of a cave, hidden, recognized by higher

perception only, Christ in the circle of the twelve, revealing
Himself as the spiritual centre of the universe, mankind and
earth evolution now, on July 6, 1948 years ago.

III.

The following translation of the Magna Charta of the Church,
although verbal, attempts to penetrate the deeper meaning of
some words. Some expressions which, in their traditional form,
are no longer accessible to modern consciousness, which may be
misunderstood, are interpreted and placed in parentheses.
When Jesus, however, came into the district of Caesarea
Philippi, He asked His spirit disciples and said:
Who do men say that the Son of Man is? -
They said:
- Some think you are John the Baptist, others,
Elijah, again others say Jeremiah or one of the
Prophets.
But He said:
- But you, who do you say that I am? -
Then Simon Peter answered and said:
- SY EI HO CHRISTOS HO HYIOS TOU THEOU TOU ZONTOS -
- YOU ARE THE CHRIST, THE SON OF THE LIVING GOD -

Jesus answered and said to them:
- Founded in yourself (blessed) are you, Simon bar-Jona,
for flesh and blood (which works out from the soul forces
and the blood) has not revealed this to you, but my
Father who lives in the heavens (in the spirit grounds
of the whole world). And I tell you: you are Peter
(who has struck the rock-ground of being) and on this
rock I will build my ECCLESIA (my spirit-called community
of men); and the gates of the underworld will not subdue it.

I will give you the keys of the kingdom of the heavens (the
kingdom of the spirit worlds); and whatever you bind on earth,
shall be bound in spirit worlds, and whatever you loose on
earth, shall be loosed in spirit worlds. -

At that time He impressed with severity upon His spirit
disciples, that they should not let anybody know that He
himself was the Christ. (Matt.16,13-20)

Whoever attentively receives this Gospel-report and tries
to relive that day's events will himself experience the release
of the extreme tension, the eruption of a burning fire, a
fire trial to be endured.

Who is able today to comprehend what this means?: One
digs into the depths and in doing so suddenly reaches the
graniteground; an experience of shock and wonder? The CHRIST!
The Messiah, expected for innumerable generations? Yes, HERE
and NOW He suddenly lights up in that Rabbi of Nazareth, Jesus,
who always speaks of himself as the "Son of Man"! Who can
comprehend the abyss opening up at this moment in the soul of
Simon bar-Jona, pointing towards an infinite horizon which
appear before him?

Into this awsome wonder of Simon the word of the just
recognized Christ-Messiah penetrates; that word which gives
him his new name referring to the "rock". Now the EKKLESIA
can be proclaimed.

IV.

First we have to deal with the following question: WHO
and WHAT is this rock? This text from the New Testament -
the Magna Charta of the Church - is not accidentally the
most important quotation in the entire history of the Church,

dividing the spirits! It seems that the history of the Church represents a continuous misunderstanding of this revelation, even when seen as a necessary element of development.

Foremost in this problem is the self-understanding of the Roman Catholic Church and how this understanding is based on the interpretation that Peter himself, in persona, is the rock on which the Church was built, especially because the name Peter, which Christ had given him, referred to this very rock. That this Peter also became the "Prince of the Apostles," the first bishop of Rome, which was the capitol of the Roman Empire in those days, brings about the primacy over all Christianity, which the Bishops of Rome who followed Peter as "Papae" (fathers) lay claim to this day. The "Apostolic Succession," i.e. the sequence of the Roman Popes beginning with Peter, certainly exists as spiritual reality. Even the list of names beginning with Peter and his first successor Linus up to the present pope need not be a forgery.

But the interpretation that Peter himself, as a person, was the rock on which the Church was founded, asks for a continuation and transfer of this task to "personal" followers of Peter. About this our fundamental word of the Gospel, however, does not speak; neither does it say that the Church as "the earthly body of Christ" was necessarily bound to Rome.

The whole course of Church history, which cannot be dealt with here, shows what grave consequences this selfinterpretation of the Roman Catholic Church and the equation of Peter and the "rock" had for the future.

The Church of the Reformation, however, developed a different understanding of this text. For them not Peter as a person is the rock on which the Church is founded but rather his confession: "You are the Christ, the Son of the Living God." On this rock on Peter's confession that He, the Christ, is the

Son of the Living God, the Church is founded. According to the understanding of the Reformation this Church exists everywhere the word of God is proclaimed purely and genuinely and the Sacraments are administered in accordance with the Scripture. The guiding principle for both is: "It is written". The sacrament, there only remain two, the Baptism and the Last Supper, in comparison with the seven sacraments of the Old Church, have lost their cultic character. Part of the lost ritual is the transsubstantiation, which however, continues to provide inner stability to the otherwise onesided Roman Church. The sermon takes the place of the rituals. Forces of reason and feeling take over the contents of "Faith" which according to Martin Luther's heartfelt statement is "an Christo hangen" (hanging on Christ). A new ortodox teaching comes about; later forces of deepened devotion again begin to stir under its frozen surface. The churches of reformation drift into many schisms. Confession remains a more or less intellectual act, carried by the will, even as far as "blind faith", for "knowledge" (Erkenntnis) is condemned from the outset and met with suspicion. Everything is based on "grace" which is bestowed "without our merits and worthiness".

Surveying the 1948 years of developing Church history since that event at Caesarea Philippi, one is able to understand the original childhood forces, born from the Mystery of Golgotha, began to fade away slowly during the first three centuries and finally died altogether. The original fiery stream of cosmic knowledge which had gushed on the disciples beginning with the event at Caesarea Philippi through Easter and Pentecost, seeped away and was slowly replaced by teachings which became more and more outmoded. Institutions took the place of the living organism of higher knowledge. The knowledge of the Gospel's mystery character was lost. Spiritual under-

standing, without which the mystery of the Epistles of Paul
cannot be grasped, was lost. The holy scriptures of the New
Covenant were faithfully collected and brought together into
a Canon, but violent intellectual battles began about their
content, fights about orthodoxy and heresy through which whole
peoples perished. The official Church no longer accepted the
genuine gnosis of Paul, of John, the school of Dionysios the
Areopagite, the Logosophy of Clement of Alexandria and Origen.
Gnosis slowly faded away into awkward systems of decadent
phantasies; what remained was the skeleton of dead dogmatism.
Knowledge (Erkenntniss) was despised and rejected.

Nevertheless from its beginning the growing of the EKKLESIA
is accompanied by a secret dream of visionary Christ-knowledge
which lights up from time to time in significant and fiery
signs, through which in many different ways the Christ-Impulse
works into the history of mankind. This spiritual fact is
nourished by the promise which Christ gave to those who belong
to Him: "Behold, I am with you till the end of the earth".
Thus the event at Caesarea Philippi on July 6,32 can be justly
connected to our time, where today the lost childhood forces
reawaken, and reawakening, open again the sources of higher
cognition. They seem to arise from the rocks, as it were, that
mankind as a whole confronts today. On these rocks of the
present, mankind is wounded even in its inmost being. Conse-
quently Man seems to lose his consciousness when dealing with
the question: what is this matter with which we are concerned?
Is matter the end and fulfillment of our existence? Or is it
the Being of the Father from which the Son arises? Will mankind in its humanity be shattered on the rocks of the materi-
alistic world outlook (Weltanschauung) or, in striking that
hard rock, will it awaken to higher vision, to the knowledge:
Christ, the Cosmic Sun Being, the Son of the Living Father,
hidden in the ground of all the world, now has become the "I"
of the earth and now fulfills His new coming in the Higher
World of unperishable life?

To the same extent as this knowledge grows, the shrine, as it were, of the scriptures which have come down to us, opens the shrine of the Christ-message in the Greek language. Its single words are surrounded by aural clouds. On these clouds His new coming takes place! Now we shall examine the words of our quotation.

V.

The first question which Jesus asks His disciples "What do men say ...? ", calls forth answers which are pertinent today, but in a different form; founder of a new religion, idealist, social revolutionary, or just a great human being, one among other heroes of mankind.

The second question "What do you say ...?", releases the lightning of suddenly opening knowledge in a flash of expanding consciousness. In this moment Simon's eyes are suddenly opened to a sight never anticipated before, his ears hear the roaring of spirit-sounds and his heart is transported into a fiery glow: YOU ARE THE CHRIST, THE SON OF THE LIVING GOD!

We may notice that this second question of Jesus begins in the present tense: "But He says"; thus it becomes a question of our time, for which we need to find the answer ourselves. We notice further that Simon does not answer "I believe", but rather, "YOU ARE..." and this is said with the powerful ex-pressiveness of the Greek: "SY EI - YOU, YOU ARE" which rela-tes to "EGO EIMI - I, I AM" which Christ uses for Himself.-This is no dogma about which one could quarrel at church councils; this is mystery language, and in the language of the mysteries Christ answers: "You are founded in yourself (blessed)"... The Greek expression "makarios", coming from "makar" (to be blessed with solid foundation,)in its deeper meaning refers to one who finds his real being, who is fulfilled in the cosmic hour of his destiny. Blessed is one who, not only in the existence after death, is grounded in himself, one "who has found his inner integrity". This throws light on how the Christ addressed Peter. In that moment of higher cognition which so suddenly came upon him, Peter grasped what gave the highest and deepest meaning to his path of life for which he was predestined. Just then he was "filled with the light of his cosmic destiny." Therefore Christ calls him by his name of destiny:

"Simon bar-Jona" ! "Schimeon" in Hebrew is the (inner) "hearing" which is open for "inspiration"; Bar-Jona means literally "brought-forth fruit (Son)" of the path of initiation of "Jona", through death and resurrection.

"Flesh and blood (sarx kai haima) have not revealed this to you", that is, neither soul forces nor what lives in the blood, neither what made him a son of the covenant of Jahveh, nor what was related to the soul-formation of the Israelitic blood stream have revealed this to you, to which the Israelite could refer when approaching his God, but "My Father who lives in the heavens". This is absolutely new, this is the rock foundation which Schimeon bar-Jona had struck in that moment. Through the remarkable relationship of this to the Christ-prayer "Pater hemon ho en tois ouranois" (Our Father who lives in the heavens) one discovers where this "rock foundation" is to be found: in the heights and depths and widths of the spirit regions, in the Fatherground of all being. The narrowness of the ego space in the "flesh and blood" of Israel, which through divine guidance concentrated in the exclusive Jahveh service, suddenly is burst open upwards,

downwards, into the widths and breadths of cosmic being: The
Father, who lives in the heavens, He just has revealed it to
you. Thus knowledge of the Father in the Son from the Holy
Spirit is the rock, the Spirit Rock, which now has consolida-
ted in the soul of Peter. Thus the eternal divine Fatherground
reaches into his "person", which now becomes able to let the
knowledge "sound through": "You are the Christ, the Son of the
living God". In this Holy Spirit-inspired moment of cognition
the Son lets Peter divine the Father. This is truth which can
be experienced and which makes free. However, one cannot pos-
sess it. One only can be "called" for this mystery-knowledge.
The one who was thus called receives a new name: "You are
Peter", you are the one who, gaining knowledge, struck the
rock foundation. "Petra" is the rock; therefore "Petros" is
not the rock itself in persona, but he who is connected with
the rock.

"... and on this rock (Petra) will I build My EKKLESIA."
In the pre-Christian Hellas "EKKLESIA" was the community of
those "called" (from ekkaleo, I call out) in order to take on
responsibility in the polis, the state. The single person was
called out of his existence as "private citizen" (idiotes) and
called upon to act in a higher sphere where the destinies of
the ethnic community were formed.

But now EKKLESIA of an entirely new kind is proclaimed:
Peter, Simon bar-Jona, who was called to higher knowledge
offers the Christ the opportunity to found His EKKLESIA on
this rock of knowledge: the community of those called out of
the transitory world conditions, the community of the free
spirits in Christo who are called to new deeds in this world.
Those spirits who gain freedom through knowing the Fatherground are to form new world destinies. This Ekklesia will be
founded on granite, as it were, on the world of matter,

newly understood from a spiritualized point of view.

Thus the very origin of the promise of the Ekklesia at
Caesarea Philippi is built on a mystery process to which, al-
ready, the following verse of the Egyptian Book of the Dead
refers: "Coming forth when hearing the voice". This verse
refers in its deeper meaning to resurrection from the grave
existence in the world of matter.

"Oikodomeszo" (I shall build), note that it is in the
future tense! Inherent is always a promise of the future:
Church is not, but will be, as it continuously grows and
transforms itself. This is the Phoenix-mystery of the Church:
again and again it enkindles the fire in order through its
death to rise rejuvenated into new life in the Christ.
"...and the gates of hell will not overcome it...", the
Greek "pylai Hadou" with its hidden image of "gates" refers
to "fortresses" of subsensible powers which know how to mani-
pulate the human beings who submit to serving them; these
powers know indeed how to extend their claim of power to the
whole of mankind. They are strong powers of temptation, which
threaten all mankind with powers of death.

A grand apocalypse is revealed in these few words which
refer to a tremendous struggle with anti-divine and anti-
spiritual powers. The Ekklesia will not live in an ivory
tower apart from the drama of world history. It is being led
through suffering, the suffering of all mankind in order to
grow strong in spirit.

Their destiny reveals the promise, again in the future tense:
"Gates of hell will not overcome it".The Greek in this context
is a special one: " kat-iszchyszouszin" is composed from the
word "iszchys", which in a sequence of seven words for
"strength or power" takes the place of the Ego-centre as
"Ego-strength". The adversary powers will not kill or over-

power the ego of the Ekklesia (ent-ichen, ueber-ichen). Surely, the struggle is about the ego! Lucifer and Ahriman are waiting to take hold of and to extinguish this ego. Through innumerable gates they proceed with their attacks. Their goal is to dehumanize and de-individualize Man through all kinds of collectivisms. The beast from the abyss represents the distorted image of Man which was forced on the thinking,feeling and willing of mankind by anti-spiritual powers.

The Ekklesia, however, the community of individualities, of called-out free spirits, is able to develop and form those powers which let mankind proceed to their goals of evolution, this belongs to the Magna Charta of the Ekklesia. It has been given the authority to meet Lucifer with an ego, strengthened through Christ, to check Ahriman through a knowledge-outlook which is trained to understand this world (Zur Welt-durch-schauung). Courage of the heart and love of the spirit give wings to this power of knowledge, which dissolves the works of Lucifer and binds the power of Ahriman.

VI.

"And I will give unto thee the keys of the kingdom of heaven". This image has slipped far too much into the sphere of egotistic concepts about the kingdom of heaven which after death will be opened to the pious; it can no longer be grasped in its deep significance. We have to make it accessible again.

Wherever we hear about "keys" in this way, gates to regions beyond our sense world are referred to. The Son of Man has "the keys of hell and of death" (Rev.1,18) and He has "the key of David, he that openeth, and no man shutteth; and shutteth and no man openeth" (Rev.3,7). The "keys" indicate the deepest secrets of destiny, essentially with the initiation into the depths and heights of the powers of being and evolving in universe, earth and Man.

It is the Christ Mystery of higher knowledge which makes available the keys to those world regions into which human thinking on the one hand is to be lifted and human willing on the other is to submerge. This refers to the task, the Magna Charta of the Church, to bind and to loosen. Strengthened thinking and enlightened willing are the essentials of the "Baszileia ton ouranon", of the Kingdom of the Heavens. Imaginative thinking binds the spirit to object and process and frees them from the bonds of Ahriman; through every act of the will, enlightened through thinking, spirit will be redeemed from the hands of Lucifer and led into new forms. Through power of thought, matter becomes condensed, through the will, loosened. Through thinking, binding activates the forming of "salt"; in willing, loosening reveals itself by the forming of "sulphur". The balance of both is brought about through "mercury" as the power of love which works in knowledge. This was how the Rosicrucians understood "binding" and "loosening".

In this we find the key-power given to the Christ-filled community of freedom-gaining spirits; what they do or do not do out of knowledge and love will bring powers of heaven into this world, so that what is bound HERE will also be bound THERE, and what is loosed HERE will also be loosed THERE.

Today the above can be explained, in "practical" terms, as follows: A natural science permeated by spiritual science, and, a spiritual science practiced according to the method of natural science that must combine in a redeeming and encompassing view of the world (Welt-Durch-Schauung), so that human world-evolution can progress, in spite of all forces of distraction. What

is needed is that courage be generated to grasp and carry
through into the future of the world that glowing stream
which secretly flows through the weave of world happenings,
the glowing stream of the living Christ.

Now we can also understand the power of binding and loosening regarding the formation of destiny. This binding and
loosening is no longer personal but gains cosmic significance.

VII.

"At that time He impressed upon His spirit disciples with
severity, that they should not let anybody know that He
Himself (autos) was the Christ."

"At that time", before the Mystery Event on Golgotha
which had to be kept secret and only later in the evolution
of mankind became an "open secret". The peoples of all nations
and races were to recognize of their own free will the being
of Christ in the being and deeds of all those who take Him
into themselves. This lives and weaves also through all those
aberrations, distortions, even in all those sins through which
Christendom became indebted to Christianity. Through the ages
the history of the Ekklesia is directed towards Christ's
Second Coming.

The great historic arc becomes noticeable in our Michaelic
Age, right in the midst of all the human catastrophies which
have shaken the century so much! It spans the history of Christianity from that event at Caesarea Philippi, 1948 years ago,
to the source of renewal in our time which grows from a truly
Christ-permeated image of man facing the "beast from the abyss".
Through the authority of the Coming-One, the new spiritual

science, the new mystery knowledge was founded by the Spirit
Teacher. In all facets of human life it offers the garment of
light to this re-appearance of Christ, through which He wants
to work. On this foundation, impulses for movements have grown,
entrusted to the deepest responsibility of those who are ready
to be "called-out" to a community of freedom-gaining spirits:
in the areas of science of knowledge, of art and religious
renewal, of education, of medicine, of agriculture, of the
threefold social organism. All these movements have begun,
as "open secrets" to permeate the conditions of this world in
"binding and loosening".

What is, after all, the Magna Charta of the Church? It is
the faculty gained through the Christ-permeated ego, to
become quietly, "binding and loosening", the salt of the earth
and the light of the world; quietly, yet freely with the courage
for responsibility, to submerge into that glowing stream of the
mysterious Christ-working and to help to support it in the
midst of a decaying world, and while doing this, to be con-
stantly prepared to transform oneself and thus also the earth.

IN MEMORIAM
Karl Friedrich Althoff
12 Nov.1980,Frankfurt/M.- 25 Feb.1980,Heiligenberg

From a rich,and fruitful life, let us mention just a few bio-
graphical details, as Karl Friedrich himself related to me during our correspondence:

Born into an atheistic family; early talent for music and
destined for a career as a concert pianist, ending with serious
illness due to heavy demand on the child's constitution.

Taught himself at the age of eleven Greek, at thirteen Hebrew,
at fourteen Arabic and Sanskrit. A reading of the Gothic version
of the Lord's Prayer led to self-chosen baptism.

He studied theology, became a student of Karl Barth. The
rise of Nazism in Germany found him in the resistance movement,
followed by arrest. Service in the Medical Corps, Prisoner of
War camp in the U.S.occupied zone. Served as Camp-Padre and
taught Greek to fellow prisoners. One of his students, Dr.Hans
Schmidt, introduced him to Anthroposophy and Karl Friedrich
found his spirit-teacher, Rudolf Steiner.

After the war, he attended the Priest-Seminar of the Chris-
tian Community in Stuttgart; worked with retarded children in
Camphill Schools in England. On his return to Germany, married
Ilse, the faithful soul-companion of his life.

In 1956, the Goethe Institute called him as lecturer, in
Germany,Egypt and, to his delight, Athens. To be able to send
his son Johannes to a Waldorf school, they returned to Germany.

After his "retirement" in 1973, an even more fruitful and
active work began. His writings on the deepest mysteries of
Christianity, the Gospels and the secrets of the genius of lan-
guages (the Prologue of the Gospel of St.John Gospel, the
Paraklete, John the Disciple, etc.) were published in several
anthroposophical publications. His great work, the Lord's
Prayer (Das Vater-Unser) Verlag Urachhaus) was published in 1978.

In the last year of his life, Ilse and Karl Friedrich built and moved into their "dreamhouse" at Heiligenberg.

A true "servant and minister of the Word" passed into the Spiritual World and from there sends his inspirations to us.

Steven Roboz